# Stay
# Safe!

## Claire Llewellyn

QEB Publishing

Library of Congress Control Number: 2005911016

ISBN 978-1-59566-195-1

Written by Claire Llewellyn
Designed by Susi Martin
Editor Louisa Somerville
Consultant Ruth Miller B.Sc., M.I.Biol., C.Biol.
Illustrations John Haslam
Photographs Michael Wicks

Publisher Steve Evans
Editorial Director Jean Coppendale
Art Director Zeta Davies

Printed and bound in China

**Picture credits**
Key: t = top, b = bottom, c = center, l = left, r = right, FC = front cover

**Gettyimages** Zen Sekizawa 16.
**Corbis** LWA-Dann Tardif/Corbis 4, / Jouval Frederique/Corbis Sygma 14.

Words in **bold** are explained

in the glossary on page 22.

# Contents

## You can do it!

When you were a baby, your parents did everything for you. They helped keep you safe.

Now that you're older, you can start to take care of yourself.

**Star tip**

As you grow, it's important to take care of your body and keep it safe.

How did these things help keep you safe when you were a baby?

crib

stair gate

safety harness

playpen

# Do it!

Find photos of yourself doing things such as singing, swimming, reading, and eating. Choose some to make a poster that shows how great your body is and what it can do.

# Home, sweet home

We spend lots of time at home. It's a place where we feel safe.

Did you know that some things around the house might harm you? It's important to take care.

**Quick quiz!**

Which of these things can be dangerous? Which help to keep us safe?

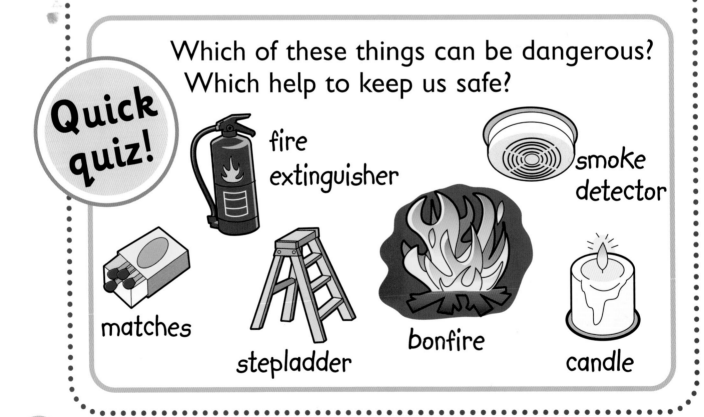

fire extinguisher

smoke detector

matches

stepladder

bonfire

candle

# Electricity

Electricity is a kind of energy that can be very **dangerous.** TVs, computers, DVD players, and lamps run on electricity. NEVER play with electric **plugs, sockets, light bulbs,** or wires.

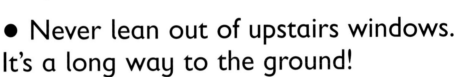

**Safety first!**

- Don't play on the stairs. It is easy to slip and fall.

- Never lean out of upstairs windows. It's a long way to the ground!

- Fire is hot and dangerous. Never play with matches or candles or go near an open fire.

## Do it!

Draw a sign that warns people of danger. What could it look like? What color should it be? Place it near something at home that you think could be a danger.

# Careful in the kitchen!

We spend lots of time in the kitchen. It's where food is kept and cooked.

Be careful when someone is cooking. Stay away from the hot oven and from pans that are on the stove.

**Watch out!**

## Knives and scissors

Many kitchen tools, such as knives and scissors, are very sharp. They are good for cutting and chopping food. Don't touch them, or you could cut yourself!

All of these things could be dangerous. Can you explain why?

iron

mug of coffee

hot soup

toaster

## Do it!

Cooking with a grownup is a good way to learn about safety in the kitchen. Do you know how to peel a potato? Can you **grate** some cheese?

# Bathroom bothers

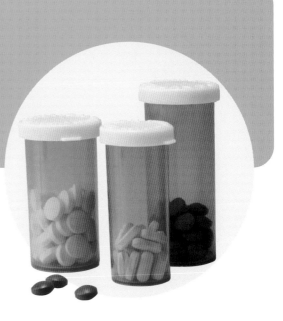

We use the bathroom to brush our teeth, use the toilet, or take a bath.

Some medicines look like candy. NEVER try to eat them.

We also keep **medicines** there. Medicines help us to feel better when we are sick.

Watch out!

## Medicines

Medicines can be dangerous. If you need medicine, an adult must give it to you. Never take it on your own.

**Safety first!**

Wet baths and floors are slippery—be careful, or you could get a bad bump.

Water can be so hot that it can burn your skin. Always test the water before you get into a bath.

Never sniff or swallow things that are used to clean the bathroom. They could make you sick and harm your body.

**Search and find!**

What can *you* *see* in this bathroom that could hurt you?

# Road safety

We all need to use the streets, but it's important to learn how to stay safe.

Cars, bikes, and trucks are heavy and fast. What could happen if one hit you?

**Watch out!**

## On the sidewalk

When you walk down the street, stay on the sidewalk and keep away from the **curb**. Walk close to the adult you are with. Keep your eyes and ears open.

## Star tip

When you go out at night, try to wear or carry something white or that glows. Then drivers can see you in the dark.

How do these help to keep people safe on the street?

car seat

bike helmet

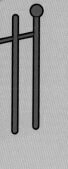

fence

reflective harness

seatbelt

## Do it!

Some people drive too fast. Make a sign that warns drivers to slow down. What picture would you put on it? What would your sign say?

Your friend wants to play soccer on the sidewalk. What do you do?

## Think about it!

# Safe crossings

Sometimes we have to cross the street. This can be tricky and needs a lot of care.

Always use **crosswalks**. They are the safest places to cross the street.

Safety first!

## Crosswalks

When you cross the street at a crosswalk, be sure to look both ways. Some crosswalks have a button that you push to make the signal change. Always wait until it's safe to cross.

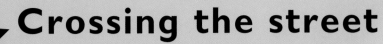

# Crossing the street

**Watch out!**

- Never cross the street by yourself.
- Wait until a grownup tells you it is safe to cross.
- Walk across the street quickly. Do not run.
- Keep your eyes and ears open for traffic.

**Think about it!**

You want to cross the street. Who can help you?

# Playing safe

It's fun going to the playground with your friends!

Be careful while you're having fun. It's easy to get hurt—and to hurt others, too.

Safety first!

- A merry-go-round spins very fast. Don't jump on or off until it stops.

- Swings are heavy and hard to stop. Don't get in their way.

- Take care on ladders and jungle gyms. If you slip, it's a long way to fall!

- Move away from the bottom of the slide. The next person could zip down really fast.

# Think about it!

A friend dares you to jump off the merry-go-round while it's still moving. What do you do?

## Star tip

Always use playground **equipment** sensibly. It's the best way to keep yourself and others safe.

**Search and find!**

Can you spot any dangers in this playground picture?

# Water warning!

It's fun to play in water on a hot summer day. But water can be very dangerous.

Be careful when you play in it.

**Watch out!**

## Water

Fish can live and breathe in water, but people can't.

If you are under water, you will need to get to the **surface** quickly to breathe in more air.

## Do it!

Go to the swimming pool at least once a week. This will help you feel at home in the water, and you will soon learn how to swim.

**Safety first!**

- Stay away from rivers, lakes, and ponds unless you're with an adult.

- Never wade or swim without an adult being nearby.

- Don't jump on or dunk your friends in the swimming pool.

**Think about it!**

You are playing in the yard with your friend when your ball lands in the pool. What do you do?

- Be careful when playing in paddling pools.

**Quick quiz!**

Where do you see these? How do they help to keep people safe?

water wings

lifeguard

kickboard

life jacket

19

# Out and about

Who keeps you safe when you're out and about: Mom, Dad or another grownup?

Stay close to them. If you don't, you could get lost, and that can be scary.

## Do it!

Learn your address and home phone number. If you get lost, this will help someone to contact your family.

7 5 3 8 2

- Strangers are people you don't know. Don't talk to strangers.

- Never take candy from strangers or go anywhere with them.

- Don't pet strange dogs. If one comes up to you, stand still and wait for it to go away.

**Star tip**

Make sure a parent or another grownup always knows where you are.

**Watch out!**

# I'm lost!

What should you do if you get lost? Ask for help right away—from a person such as a police officer or store clerk.

This will help you to stay safe.

# Glossary

**crosswalk** a safe place on the street where people who are walking can cross

**curb** the edge between a sidewalk and a street

**dangerous** something that can cause you harm

**equipment** the slides, swings, and other games at a playground

**grate** to cut things into small shreds, using a grater

**light bulb** a glass globe which gives out light when electricity passes through it

**medicine** the special liquid or pills that we take to make us well

**plug** the plastic and metal part at the end of an electrical cord that fits into a socket

**socket** a special hole into which you plug something that runs on electricity, such as a TV. A socket is usually on a wall

**surface** the top or outside of anything

# Index

# Notes
## for parents and teachers

- Look at photographs with your children of when they were babies. Ask your children to look for any safety equipment (e.g. car seat, playpen) or other ways in which they were protected.

- Discuss safety in the kitchen. Ask your children to suggest which places in the kitchen could be dangerous. Look at a variety of kitchen tools. Show the children what they are made of and the different jobs they can do.

- Ask the children to suggest all the things that could be hot in their homes. Draw pictures and label each one. Discuss the different ways children can avoid getting burned.

- Help your children to make a list of the electrical equipment they have at home. Ask them to show the list to their grandparents. How many of the items did they have in their house when they were young? Did they look/work the same?

- Visit a park or playground with your children. What safety measures are in place? Why? Discuss how accidents could happen in the playground and what steps the children can take to prevent them.

- Next time you are walking down the street with your children, discuss the best places to cross the street. Encourage them to keep their eyes and ears open. Can they spot any dangers?

- Invite a police officer into school and interview him/her about pedestrian safety. What kind of uniform does a traffic officer wear?

- Discuss with your children how shiny things reflect the light and keep us safe in the dark. Investigate reflective strips and other shiny surfaces. How and where would they expect them to shine? Try out your children's ideas to find out if they were right.

- Ask your children to think of animals that can breathe under water (or hold their breath for a very long time). Using books and the Internet, research one of these animals and write a fact sheet about it.

- Help your children to list all the different places they regularly go together—e.g. the library, park, swimming pool. Talk about what they would do if they got lost in each of these places. Who could they ask for help?